to cANineS oN a MidNighT CleAr ❧

sERve NyLa[barcode]❧ W9-BNH-709 hi[p]

HowL'd oN hiGH ❧ JoYLaNd ❧

[E]LVE dAYs of ChristMas ❧ oh, co[M]

[L]L ❧ gO, fEtCh iT On the MoUNtAiN

Ark!" we SoUNd aS angeLs SinG ❧

[h]auL yOur FEeT hArd ❧ obEY, Ma[r]

[T] BitE ❧ oLd CaNiNes ❧ Dog, REst

oN a MidNighT CleAr ❧ We giVe y[ou]

[D]oNE ❧ i saw tHRee hiPs ❧ wAg yoUr T

[G]H ❧ Look, mA, it's HaNUKkah! ❧

[i] coMe And pLaY the GaMe we K

HoLidAY HoUNDs

Traditional Songs for Festive Dogs

HoLidAY HoUNDs
Traditional Songs for Festive Dogs

bY lAURie loUgHLiN

ilLUsTrAteD bY MaRY ROSs

CHRONICLE BOOKS
San Francisco

The author and publisher have made every reasonable attempt to
determine that the songs parodied in this work are in the public
domain.

Printed in Hong Kong.

Book and cover design: Carrie Leeb, Leeb & Sons.

Library of Congress Cataloging-in-Publication Data:
Loughlin, Laurie.
Holiday hounds : traditional songs for festive dogs / by Laurie Loughlin;
illustrations by Mary Ross.
p. cm.
Parodies of Christmas Songs (principally) ; includes some for Hanukkah.
ISBN: 0-8118-1432-7
1. Christmas music—Texts. 2. Christmas—Humor. 3. Hanukkah—Songs and music—Texts.
4. Hanukkah—Humor. 5. Dogs—Humor. 6. Dogs—Songs and music. 7. Parodies. I. Title.
M1629.3.C5L68 1996
782.42'1723'0268—dc20   96-1838
                                                         CIP
                                                         MN

Distributed in Canada by Raincoast Books
8680 Cambie Street
Vancouver, B.C. V6P 6M9

10 9 8 7 6 5 4 3 2 1

Chronicle Books
275 Fifth Street
San Francisco, CA 94103

Chronicle Books® is registered in the U.S. Patent
and Trademark Office.

For my aunt and uncle, Doris and Bill
Brennan, and their dogs Emma Rose, who still
woofs with us, and Buford and Charley, who
bark with the angels now.

I want to thank

* all my relatives and friends who told tales

* Alice and Sam Shannon for the use
of their doggone library

* and my Canine Chorale: Charlotte Bingham,
Grendel Chang, Princess Genevieve Smitha Green,
Chanda Mae and Mickey Mouse Hallsted, Chelsea
and P. J. Laifer, Misty O'Brien, Ivan and Sasha
Peiser, B. J. Rollins, Zachary Scutt, Taily-po
Sexton, Woody Sholar, and Panda Strang Todd.

tABLE of

coNtentS

Dog, rest Ye Merry, Gentle One

Dog, rest ye merry, gentle one,
And when you wake, we'll play.
Then you can jump on all the guests
Who come for Christmas Day,
And save us all from feeling sad
If our thoughts go astray,
Oooh, guardian of comfort and joy,
Comfort and joy,
Oooh, guardian of comfort and joy.

("God Rest Ye Merry, Gentlemen")

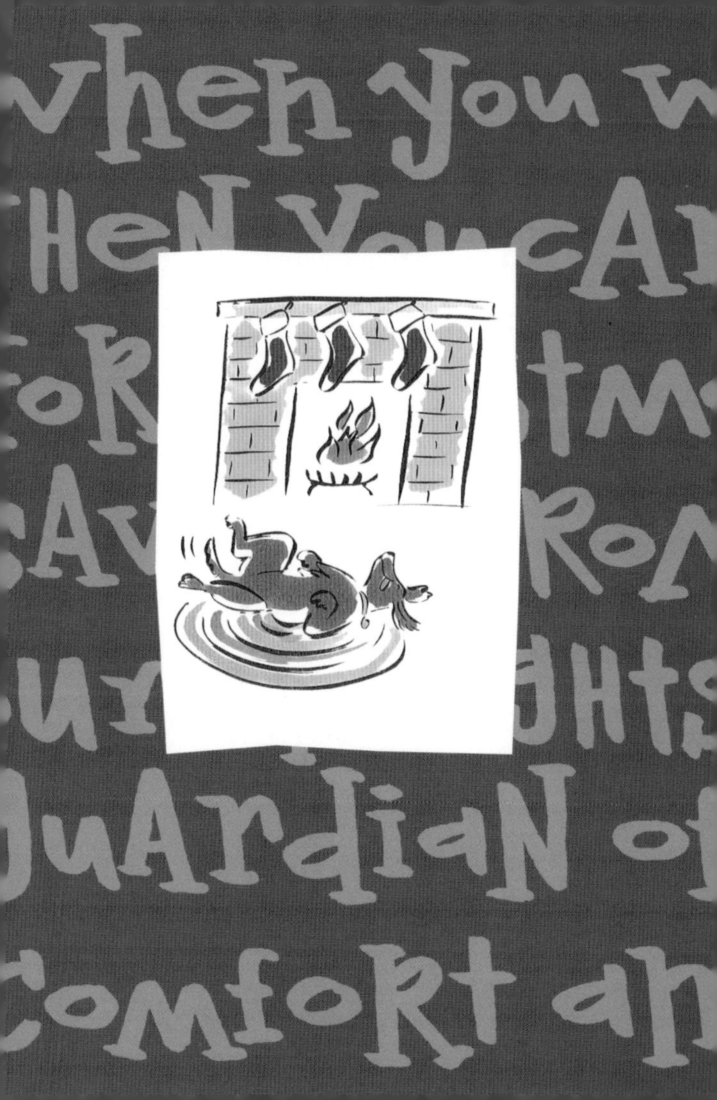

to cAnines oN
a MidNighT cLeAr

To canines on a midnight clear
A glorious tale was told,
Of how their ancestors saved the day
One Christmas Eve of olde.
When Santa's sack slipped off the roof
With presents falling free,
Those loyal dogs picked up all the gifts
And dropped them under the tree.

("It Came Upon a Midnight Clear")

WE gIVE YoU
OUr ChriStmas wish LiSt

We give you our Christmas wish list.
We give you our Christmas wish list.
We give you our Christmas wish list
For a Happy New Year.

Good buyings to you
Wherever you shop,
Good buyings for Christmas
And a Happy New Year!

("We Wish You a Merry Christmas")

SERVE NYLABONE Serve,
serve Nylabone.
and all year long,
It cleans my teeth
and underneath.
really great 🦴 From
through day eight
Serve, serve Nyla
Holidays and all

serve, serve, serve,
For Hanukkah
all year long.
Both on top
And it tastes
day one right

("Sov S'Vivon")

bone
year long!

i saw tHReE hips

I saw three hips come tailing in
On Christmas Day, on Christmas Day.
I saw three hips come tailing in
On Christmas Day, in the morning.

On other dogs who came my way
On Christmas Day, on Christmas Day.
On other dogs who came my way
On Christmas Day, in the morning.

I circled each one warily
On Christmas Day, on Christmas Day.
I circled each one warily
On Christmas Day, in the morning.

And knocked their hips as they passed by
On Christmas Day, on Christmas Day.
And knocked their hips as they passed by
On Christmas Day, in the morning.

To let them know the boss was I
On Christmas Day, on Christmas Day.
To let them know the boss was I
On Christmas Day, in the morning.

("I Saw Three Ships")

WAG YOUR TAILS

Wag your tails at food approaching.
Bow Wow! Wow! Wow! Wow! . . . Wow!
Wow! Wow! Wow!
Little pups, you need some coaching.
Bow Wow! Wow! Wow! Wow! . . . Wow!
Wow! Wow! Wow!
Stand on hind legs and start barking.
Bow Wow! Wow! Wow! Wow! Wow! . . .
Wow! Wow! Wow!
On a dog's life you're embarking.
Bow Wow! Wow! Wow! Wow! . . . Wow!
Wow! Wow! Wow!

("Deck the Halls")

Engines, We Have Howl'd on High

Engines, we have howl'd on high.
To your sirens we respond,
As the trucks go rushing by,
Echoing in unison.

Aouuuuuuuuuuuuuuuuuuuuuu. Aouu.
In accord we bay. Oh,
Aouuuuuuuuuuuuuuuuuuuuuu. Aouu.
In accord we ba-ay, oh.

("Angels We Have Heard on High")

JoYLaNd

Joyland, joyland,
Hints can turn life to ployland.
When I grab my food dish,
They may fill it full at once.

Doggie ployland,
Please make my life a joyland.
If I roll my big brown eyes,
They may give me what I want.

("Toyland")

Look, Ma, it's Hanukkah!

When winter blankets our yard
And bright menorahs shine proudly in the dark,
Bright menorahs shine proudly in the dark,
We puppies all yelp with glee.
We puppies all yelp with glee.
We puppies all yelp with glee,
"Look, Ma, it's Hanukkah!"

When dreidels roll on the floor
And plates of latkes come through the kitchen
door,
Plates of latkes come through the kitchen door,
We share the news right away.
We share the news right away.
We share the news right away,
"Look, Ma, it's Hanukkah!"

("Lichvod Ha Chanukah")

24

The twElve dAys
of ChristMas

(After singing each couplet, in reverse order repeat the second line of all previous couplets.)

On the first day of Christmas, my owner gave to me
A puppy for company.

On the second day of Christmas, my owner gave to me
Two water bowls and

On the third day of Christmas, my owner gave to me
Three King Kongs,

On the fourth day of Christmas, my owner gave to me
Four fleecy rugs,

On the fifth day of Christmas, my owner gave to me
Five latex toys . . .

On the sixth day of Christmas, my owner gave to me
Six rhinestone collars,

On the seventh day of Christmas, my owner gave to me
Seven safety sitters,

On the eighth day of Christmas, my owner gave to me
Eight Kanine Krispies,

On the ninth day of Christmas, my owner gave to me
Nine grooming brushes,

On the tenth day of Christmas, my owner gave to me
Ten Wag Bag pet beds,

On the eleventh day of Christmas, my owner gave to me
Eleven chewy breath mints,

On the twelfth day of Christmas, my owner gave to me
Twelve tag reflectors,

("The Twelve Days of Christmas")

Oh, come and play

so well, ❧ Inquisit

show-and-tell. ❧ ❧

Christmas suitcase

Our findings to the

guest we'll drag. ❧

I've snatched a shoe

retrieved the wallet

the game we know

ive dog brand of

We'll poke the

and bag.

honored

Rejoice! Rejoice!

to tear! ❧ And you've

with great flair!

gO, fEtCh iT
On the MoUNtaiN

When I was a puppy,
They'd take me out to play.
They'd spin a flying saucer
In air, and then they'd say,

CHORUS:
"Go, fetch it on the mountain,
Over the hill, in fields of corn.
Go, fetch it on the mountain.
Our Frisbee King is born."

I could run like lightning
And catch it on a dime.
I'd bring it back. They'd pat me
And throw it one more time.

CHORUS:
"Go, fetch it on the mountain,
Over the hill, in fields of corn.
Go, fetch it on the mountain.
Our Frisbee King is born."

("Go, Tell It on the Mountain")

WHeN i wa

HEY'd taKE

Spi   Yi

ANd   t

etch it oN t

Er the hil

oN the Mou

TheSe thREe cArs
of OrieNT aRe

These three cars of Orient are
Honda, Nissan, and Toyota.
Westward down our street we chase them,
Spurring their travel far. Oooh . . .

CHORUS:
Bark at tires! Bark at hood!
Scare the fenders! Scare 'em good!
We protect our territory
Like all able guard dogs should.

Our families run out and blurt,
"Don't you do that! You could get hurt."
While they leave us free to wander,
We're always on alert. Oooh . . .

(Repeat CHORUS)

These three cars, temptations they reek,
Cruising every day of the week.
We're united, get excited,
And down the road we streak. Oooh . . .

(Repeat CHORUS)

("We Three Kings of Orient Are")

"ʙArk!" we SouNd aS anɢeʟs SinG

"Bark!" we sound as angels sing.
Harmony's a lovely thing.
They use wings, and we use jowls.
They have harps, and we have howls.

Joyful as our rations rise!
Christmas dinner! Christmas pies!
When we're feeling this darned good,
We serenade the neighborhood.

"Bark!" we sound as angels sing.
Harmony's a lovely thing.

("Hark! The Herald Angels Sing")

auNt Fay's hARMONica

In my younger days we had a custom
At Hanukkah to congregate each night.
Relatives would all come here to our house,
And I would yip and pant with great delight.

We loved songs of victory and tradition.
The family would sing, and I would howl.
We didn't have a guitar or piano,
But we could keep the tempo anyhow.

CHORUS:
Aunt Fay's harmonica! Aunt Fay's harmonica!
Providing rhythm for our favorite rhymes,
So shiny and so gold, so full of little holes,
So instrumental to our happy times.

While the celebration was in progress,
I would visit many different laps.
The only problem with these lovely parties
Was noise preventing me from taking naps.

Aunt Fay was an expert with the scale notes.
Her face puffed up with gusto when she played.
It got real late, but no one ever noticed.
They all kept shouting, "Mazel tov!" and stayed.

(Repeat CHORUS)

("Eight Days of Chanukah")

LEt me hauL
Your FEeT HArd

Let me haul your feet hard.
Can I run with you?
Here's a path.
Let's whisk around a time or two.
Clinging to my leash
Will be a challenge true.
Let me haul your feet hard.
Can I run with you?

(a.k.a The Big Dogs' Song)

("Let Me Call You Sweetheart"
—for Valentine's Day)

38

obEY, Maria

"Obey, Maria."
That is what my teachers say
In obedience school each day.
I do my best to please. I do.
I walk in circles round the park
Putting left foot first to start.
I come off the leash
Because I've learned all the commands.
"Come. Heel, Maria.
Sit. Stay, Maria, Maria."

Here's my diploma.
This is graduation day!
I have made my family so proud,
All the people clapping.
I'm in! I'm in!

("Ave Maria")

wHaT ChILD iS THiS?

What child is this who, laid to rest
Upon her bed, is sleeping?
I love her so and snuggle close.
While Christmas dawns, she's dreaming.

This is the little girl
Who rubs my belly and combs my curls.
Most precious in all the world,
I've heard them call her Mary.

("What Child Is This?")

42

SILENT BITE Silent bit

All is gone. Thr

Christmas goodie

I, in weakness, com

Swallowed all in

Swallowed all in

e. Whole-ee bite.

oat feels tight.

on countertop left.

mitted the theft,

one piece,

("Silent Night")

one piece.

oLd caNiNEs

Should old of great stance be forgot
And never brought to hind?
Should old of great stance be forgot
And days of old canines?
Four old canines are here,
Four old canines.
We'll raise our tails
As New Year's hails
Four old canines!

("Auld Lang Syne"—for New Year's Eve)

Dog, Rest Ye Merry, Gentle One

We give you Our Christmas wish Lis

Wag your Tails ❖ Engines, We H

ook, ma, it's Hanukkah! ❖ The

And play the Game we Know So

These three cars of Orient are ❖

aunt Fay's Harmonica ❖ Let m

❖ what Child is this? ❖ Sile

Ye Merry, Gentle One ❖ to Canin

r Christmas wish List ❖ Serve Ny

Engines, We Have Howl'd on

he twElve Days of Christmas ❖